MEASURING TEMPERATURE

By Julia Vogel • Illustrated by Luanne Marten

The Child's World®

Published by The Child's World®
1980 Lookout Drive • Mankato, MN 56003-1705
800-599-READ • www.childsworld.com

Acknowledgments
The Child's World®: Mary Berendes, Publishing Director
The Design Lab: Cover and interior design
Amnet: Cover and interior production
Red Line Editorial: Editorial direction

Photo credits
Morgan Lane Photography/Shutterstock Images, cover, 1, 2; Shutterstock Images,
cover, 1; Jani Bryson/iStockphoto, 5; iStockphoto, 6, 19; Michael C. Gray/
Shutterstock Images, 11; Sergej Razvodovskij/Shutterstock Images, 14;
Gary Whitton/Shutterstock Images, 16; Rob Marmion/Shutterstock Images, 21

ISBN 9781614732808
LCCN 2012933668

Printed in the United States of America
Mankato, MN
July 2012
PA02121

ABOUT THE AUTHOR

Award-winning author Julia Vogel spent many cold New England winters earning a doctorate in forestry. Julia has four kids, a dog that loves snow, and three cats that love sleeping in warm sunshine.

ABOUT THE ILLUSTRATOR

Luanne Marten has been drawing for a long time. She earned a bachelor's degree in art and design from the University of Kansas. Luanne loves to draw on cold and hot days.

TABLE OF CONTENTS

Hot or Cold?

What should you wear today? Knowing if it is hot or cold outside will probably help you decide.

You might have all sorts of questions about hot and cold. Is that hot chocolate too hot to drink? Is your little sister feeling sick? How can you answer these questions? By measuring **temperature**!

Knowing the temperature helps you figure out if you should wear a hat to stay warm.

People had to guess how hot an oven was before there was a way to measure temperature.

How to Tell?

Long ago, people did not know how to measure temperature. They had to guess. That made many jobs hard. A hot oven can bake bread. But a too-hot oven will burn it.

It was hard to tell exactly how hot or cold it was outside. That made planning for outside work difficult, too. People needed a way to find out how hot or cold things were.

Thermometers to the Rescue

About 500 years ago, scientists went to work. They knew that alcohol and some other liquids **expand** when they get warmer. The liquids **contract** when they cool down. Scientists made glass tubes and put the liquids inside. These were the first **thermometers**.

The first thermometers looked very different from our thermometers today.

When people measure things, they often use a **unit**. For temperature, the unit is a **degree**. Degrees are noted with a little circle (°).

Soon, marks divided the old-fashioned thermometers into degrees. The liquid inside rose and fell as it heated or cooled. The top of the liquid lined up with a degree mark. The mark told the temperature.

The temperature on this thermometer is about 80°.

Two people could measure hot water and get two different temperatures.

Standard Scales

The first thermometers were very different from the ones we use today. Imagine two people measuring the temperature of the same water with different thermometers. One person might get 40°. The other might get 60°. It was confusing.

Scientist Daniel Fahrenheit figured out how to fix this. In the early 1700s, he made a standard scale for temperature. He set one end of the scale at the freezing point of water. It is 32° Fahrenheit, or 32°F. He set the other end of the scale at the boiling point of water. It is 212°F.

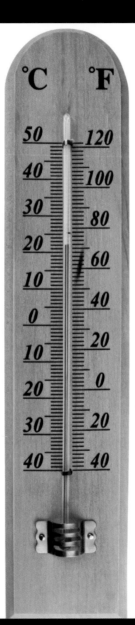

°C   °F

50   120
40   100
30   80
20   60
10   40
0   20
10   0
20   20
30   30
40   40

The Celsius scale has fewer numbers than the Fahrenheit scale.

KNOW THE SCALE
Fahrenheit and Celsius temperature numbers are usually different. You need to know which scale you're using to make sense of temperatures. Imagine it is 30° outside. If it 30°C, you could go swimming. But if it is 30°F, you could go ice-skating.

Fahrenheit's thermometer worked well. But it was hard to remember the freezing point was 32° and the boiling point was 212°. Anders Celsius developed a simpler scale. He set the freezing point of water at 0° Celsius, or 0°C. He set the boiling point at 100°C.

Scientists and most countries around the world use Celsius. The United States and a few other places use Fahrenheit.

What is the temperature of this cold winter day?

HOTTEST AND COLDEST The hottest temperature recorded in the United States was in Death Valley, California, in 1913. It was 134°F, or 56.7°C. The coldest temperature was in Prospect Creek, Alaska, in 1971. It was −79.8°F, or −62.1°C.

Measuring Mania

How hot is it where you live? Set up an outdoor thermometer to find out. The liquid will rise in the tube on a hot summer day. What is the temperature in degrees Fahrenheit and Celsius?

How cold does it get for you in the winter? Is it cold enough to snow? Remember, it needs to be 32°F, or 0°C, for rain to turn into frozen flakes. In some places, temperatures can drop below 0° on both scales. Then the temperatures are negative numbers. It might be −5°F, or −20.5°C. When you see negative temperatures, it's time to go inside!

Thermometers are inside your home, too. They help keep you safe and comfortable. A thermometer on the furnace helps keep your house warm all winter. A thermometer on the water heater stops your shower from getting too hot.

Thermometers help you cook in the kitchen. A thermometer in the refrigerator lets you make sure your milk and leftovers stay cool. A thermometer in the oven helps make sure you don't burn your pizza.

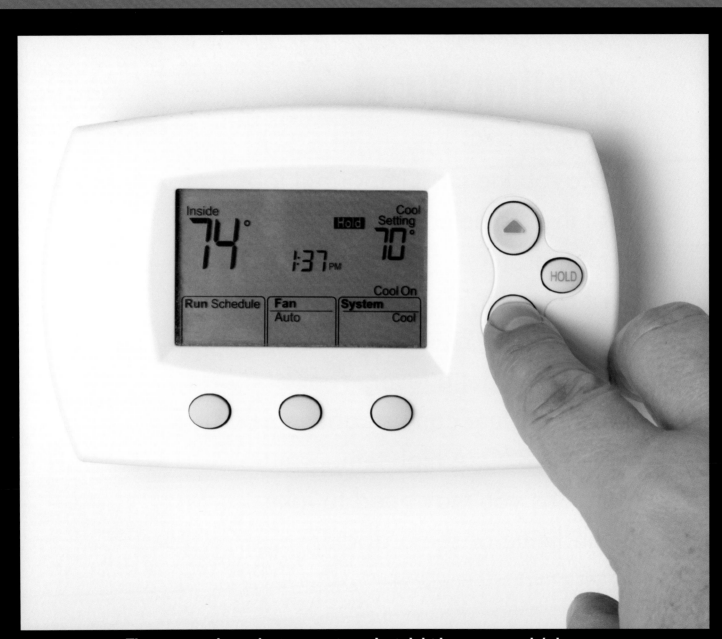

Thermostats keep the temperatures just right in many people's homes.

Feeling Warm

Maybe the most important job of thermometers is checking our temperatures. Body temperature of a healthy person is 98.6°F, or 37°C. But sometimes when you're sick, you get a fever. Your body temperature can rise above 100°F, or 37.8°C. A high temperature means you may need to take medicine or see a doctor.

TAKE YOUR TEMPERATURE
Do you have a thermometer at home? Ask if you can take your temperature. What is it?

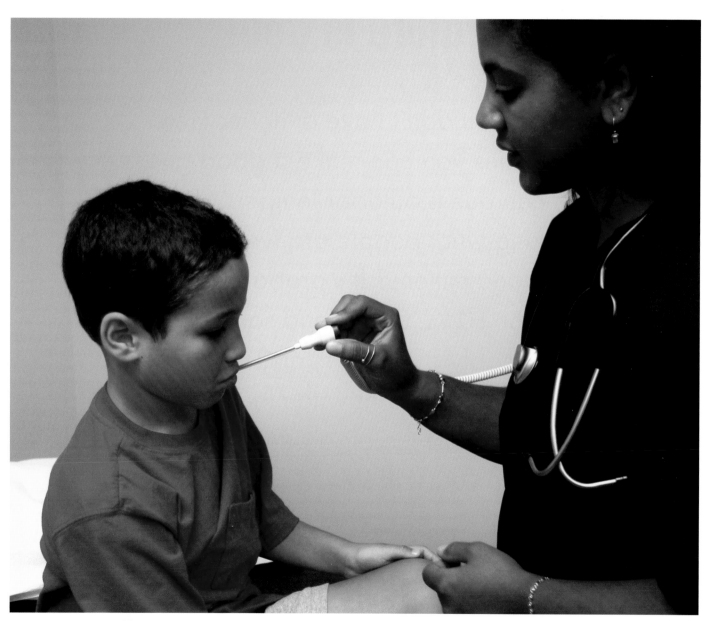

You probably have had your temperature taken at the doctor's office.

Temperature Is Cool

What if you don't have a thermometer?
Sometimes you can make a good guess.
You can guess outdoor temperature by
checking what people are wearing.
Coats and mittens? It's probably less than
50°F, or 10°C. Shorts and sandals?
It's probably over 75°F, or 23.9°C.

Now you know how to measure the
temperature of the air around you, your food,
and even yourself! What is the temperature
of the milk in your refrigerator or the pond
by your house? Grab your thermometer and
start measuring!

If you see people outside with coats, hats, and mittens, it is probably cold weather.

Glossary

contract (kuhn-TRAKT): If things contract, they get smaller. Some liquids contract when they get colder.

degree (di-GREE): A degree is a unit of measure for temperature. A degree lets people understand different temperatures around the world.

expand (ik-SPAND): If things expand, they get larger. Some liquids expand when they get hotter.

temperature (TEM-pur-uh-chur): Temperature is the measurement of how hot or cold something is. Knowing the temperature outside helps you decide what to wear.

thermometers (thur-MAH-mi-turs): Thermometers are tools used to measure temperature. Thermometers are inside and outside of homes.

unit (YOU-nit): A unit is a standard amount used to measure. A degree is a unit for measuring temperature.

Books

Kensler, Chris. *Secret Treasures and Magical Measures Revealed: Adventures in Measuring.* New York: Simon & Schuster, 2003.

Moore, Rob. *Why Does Water Evaporate? All about Heat and Temperature.* New York: PowerKids Press, 2010.

Woodford, Chris. *Temperature.* San Diego, CA: Blackbirch Press, 2005.

Web Sites

Visit our Web site for links about measuring temperature: **childsworld.com/links**

Note to Parents, Teachers, and Librarians: We routinely verify our Web links to make sure they are safe and active sites. So encourage your readers to check them out!

Index